HEAVENLY INSPIRATIONS

Debbie Girard

Dedication

I would like to thank my family and friends for all their support. I love you all, and God bless you. I dedicate this to all of you.

Acknowledgment

I want to thank the Lord for giving me the talent to write. I thank You, Lord, and give You all praise.

Moving out to minister and touch lives is scary at first, but if it is God's will, it will flow with the fullness of the Spirit. You will be guided and led to do that which you must do; just remember to be obedient. His power is stronger than any other out there. God is great!!!

Be at peace. Listen for His voice. He is there with you.

About the Author

Debbie lives in Pennsylvania. She is married with three adult children and their spouses. She has six grandchildren. She also has a pet shorkie that she adores. Debbie enjoys nature and its' beauty. She has been writing poetry for many years. She is active in her church and loves the Lord. She has also been active volunteering in her community.

Table of Contents

This Is The Life For Me

This is the life for me,

Living for God.

This is the life for me,

Living for God.

He takes my hand and leads me,

To a place where I'll be free.

This is the life for me,

Living for God.

Debbie Girard

Love So True

The Lord has bound us together,

To share God's Word with you.

The Lord has bound us together,

To tell you of a life that's new.

His love just pours on down,

Like a sparkling morning dew.

So let it fall on down,

To touch each one of you.

He loves each one of us,

And we all love you too.

So let's all bind together,

In a love so true.

Look Up

I looked out my window, and what did I see,

But pain and sorrow and strife.

I looked up in the sky, and what did I see,

But glory and grace and life.

So many times, we look out and not up,

And that's where trouble begins.

But when we look up and not out,

That's when the victories come in.

If we simply close our eyes when we look out,

And pray for what is there,

Then we begin looking up and the out is no longer there.

So let's lift our eyes to where they should be,

Then the out that was there we no longer will see.

Debbie Girard

He Chose Me

Sometimes I sit and wonder, 0 Lord, why did you choose me?

I am so far from being what you would want me to be.

I feel like I'm lost in a dark, crowded forest,

I feel like a non-blooming flower among many beautiful blossoms.

I wonder, 0 Lord, should I keep going on?

Then I remember Your Word when you said you have chosen me,

I remember your Son on Mount Calvary.

I know that in time, my blossoms will show,

And they'll be more beautiful than anyone can know.

Thank you Lord for choosing me,

Now use me lord for what you want me to be.

I'll Follow You

Sometimes I feel so down and low,

I just don't know which way to go.

I feel such an aching deep down within,

I don't know where I'm going and not sure where I've been.

I feel like a body without a soul,

Like I have no future, I have no goal.

But oh, when I set my eyes on the Lord and begin to pray,

How quickly those feelings begin to fade away.

I begin searching and looking, wanting and hoping,

For the many wonderful things that the Lord can bring.

He turns my sadness into gladness, my confusion into light,

My hurt into laughter, my lowness into new heights.

I feel excited and full to overflowing,

And then I realize I know where I'm going.

I'll follow the Lord and obey Him fully,

Even though some others may treat me cruelly.

Debbie Girard

I'll go where He wants me to go,

do what He wants me to do, Lord I live to truly serve You.

Give Me Strength

The hurt, the pain, the sorrow,

Sometimes I wonder if it's worth it all.

I ache deep down within,

An ache I can't explain.

I cry with silent tears that fall, and lay upon my cheek.

Oh I wonder if I should go on, or just stop and take defeat.

The battle scars can sometimes cut way deep into the heart.

O Lord I pray for your grace, please take the hurt away.

Your power can overcome the pain, and victory can come my way.

I don't want to give up, I want to march on,

Please, Lord give me the strength to sing a victory song.

To let the hurt disappear, to heal my aching heart.

O Lord I want to feel the joy,

That your love can put in my soul.

I cry out loud, I cry out strong,

Lord set me free, your face to see.

Debbie Girard

When with no one else my thoughts I can share,

Lord I know you'll always be there.

Miracles Can Happen

As I sat in the warmth of my home one night,

Outside it was sleeting and snowing.

Then out of nowhere, there came thunder and lightning.

Now isn't that strange to have that when it's snowing?

The more I sat and thought on this, I began to understand.

You see, we will believe that we saw lightning cause our eyes

showed us it was there.

We will believe there was thunder cause we heard it echo in our ears.

It was a miracle, something that normally doesn't happen.

A sign to show us miracles do take place, that we should believe.

And if we believe in these miracles even though we don't

understand,

No matter how big or small they would seem, they're miracles,

one and all.

We would see great things happen around us.

Remember, if it can thunder and lightning while it's snowing in the

Debbie Girard

winter,

Miracles can happen anytime, anywhere,

So believe in them cause they're already there

The Light Will Shine

As the moon shines bright on a silent night,

So the Lords' light shines on you.

So it is with you when you feel surrounded by darkness.

Though troubles and circumstances seem to be mighty,

Pray and the Lords' light will brighten your way.

The darkness will lift and fade away,

And the light will shine so bright about you,

That darkness will be gone and never be found.

Debbie Girard

In His Hand

As I looked up in the sky one day,

I saw a cloud, only one in the sky.

There was not another cloud to be seen.

To me this stood for the One and Only.

And as the cloud turned in the sky,

It looked like a hand reaching into the heavens.

It made me think of reaching out,

To praise His Holy name.

It also made me think of Him,

And how He puts us in the palm of His hand.

To care for each and every one of us.

And if we continue to serve and live for Him,

He will keep us in His loving hands.

Words

Lord help each and every one of us,

That our words will be pure as gold.

That no matter what we speak,

Our mouths may be truly controlled.

Please guide us to lean toward that perfection,

That will make us more like you.

Let not a word pass our lips,

That would hurt another soul.

But let each and every word we say,

Lead another to living for you today.

Words don't seem like very much,

Until someone else they may touch.

Debbie Girard

Teach Me Lord

Lord, I love You,

Guide me Your way.

Teach me each day,

To do what You would have me to do.

Forgive me Lord for the wrong I've done.

I want to strive to be like You.

To love and care, to do and share.

To bring others to Your wonderful love.

That they also may share that eternal life.

Lord, through You, and only You,

Can I be that obedient vessel that I should be.

Through You all mighty and marvelous miracles can be done

Lord, this is Your day, lead me Your way.

Forgiven

My sins were so many, how could I ask,

That the Lord would forgive my terrible past.

Then I looked in His Word and He told me,

My sins are all forgiven:

He removed them as far as the east is from the west.

All I have to do is ask Him in my heart,

Forgive me of all my sins,

And believe in Him.

And then He spoke to me and said,

"Your sins are forgiven, my child,

They are under the blood and washed away.

So if I forgive you, then you can forget them."

He set me free and cleansed my soul,

My Savior made me whole.

Debbie Girard

Giving

I looked out once at a great big tree,

And there was a man standing, I did see.

He was grabbing the leaves and putting them in a great big pile.

Then he took this pile and put them in a big sack,

And carried them off upon his back.

I looked out again at the great big tree,

And another man there I did see.

He was taking the leaves right off the tree,

But he had no pile that I could see.

For as he took the leaves from there,

He handed them out to others with care.

Now stop and think what you would do,

Well, let's just put it into view.

Do you want to be like the man who puts them in a sack,

Who takes them away while others lack.

For do you know what will happen to those leaves he has?

They will all rot and be a part of the past.

What did he gain by doing this task?

He gave nothing and got nothing back.

But you see, the man who is giving those leaves away,

He's bringing joy to others in a very special way.

So you see he is getting cause he's giving away,

So that others may have better, brighter days.

Now, maybe you know what you'd rather be,

Someone who keeps what he has but gains nothing you see.

Or someone who shares and brings joy to others every day,

And gains more each day with what he has given away.

Debbie Girard

Spring Is Near

This is the time of year,

When we know spring is very near.

We think of warmth and the sun,

We think about all the work to be done.

We think about the flowers that bloom,

And how they smell like a sweet perfume.

But I like to think of who created what's here,

And how He held each thing so dear.

I take one flower and pause to look,

To see its' creation and what care it took.

With the time He took with the flowers and trees,

I know He must care for you and me.

For with the blossoms and everything new,

He offers a new life for me and you.

For if we let Him in our heart,

That's where our new life begins to start.

We'll have a life with Him someday,

Something that no one can take away.

So in this time when spring is near,

Let's think of the one who put it here.

As new life comes to the flowers and things,

Let's thank God for all He brings,

For all of nature that we see,

And for that home in eternity.

Debbie Girard

He Died For You And Me

There is something so precious, you see,

What Jesus did for you and me.

He knew beforehand what He must do,

Because He so loved me and you.

He suffered that day for you and me,

As He died on the cross of Calvary.

A crown of thorns upon His head,

As to Galgotha He was led.

To that cross they nailed His hands,

Those hands that had healed in all the lands.

The pain He must have felt just then,

For all of us and all our sin.

The bitter wine He had to drink,

Now doesn't this make you stop and think.

How much He loves us, each one,

To do what He knew must be done.

He died on that cross for you and me,

So we would have a chance for life eternally.

Debbie Girard

Look Unto Me

I say look only unto Me,

That's where the blessings you will see.

Just call upon My precious name,

I was and always will be the same.

I'll guide you with each step you take,

The right decision together we'll make.

Through you others may see Me,

To bring in that great victory.

We together can do it right,

To bring this world a bright new light.

So always call upon My name,

Remember that's where your blessings came.

Can't You Feel It

Can't you feel it in the air,

Can't you feel it everywhere?

It's with you every step you take,

When you're asleep or awake.

It's there to help you every day,

As you go down life's pathway.

This is the gift sent from above,

The Holy Spirit from Jesus' love.

Debbie Girard

A True Peace

There is a peace for you,

It's fresh as the morning dew.

A peace that's deep within,

With the forgiveness of your sins.

Let Jesus in your heart today,

Your sins and burdens to Him lay.

And He will set you free.

Then you will really know and see,

There is a true peace from up above,

Because of Jesus's precious love.

Beautiful Nature

The sky is shining a bright blue,

The trees are blossoming with life anew.

The flowers are all beginning to grow,

And soon all their beauty will show.

How beautiful nature is to see,

What wonder God created for you and me.

The birds sing their sweet song,

As the sun shines all day long.

Look at nature carefully,

There is something special to see.

It can make you smile when you feel down,

And thank the Lord for the beauty around.

Debbie Girard

A Family Wept

A family wept beside the bed,

They knew within, their daughter was dead.

At her bedside, they did weep,

But Jesus said she's just asleep.

They laughed at Him and didn't believe,

So Jesus asked them all to leave.

He held her hand so small and mild,

And said, "Arise, oh my child."

Then as that little girl did raise,

Her parents stood there, just amazed.

So do not fear and just believe,

The miracles then you can't conceive.

Ref. Luke 8:40-56

Feeding The Multitude

The apostles and Jesus were in a deserted place,

The multitudes found out and came to see His face.

He spoke of God and His kingdom,

Healing those who to Him did come.

But towards the end of the day,

The apostles told Jesus to send the multitudes away.

For they need food and a place to stay,

And we don't have enough to feed the five thousand today.

What do you have, was what Jesus said,

They replied, two fish and five loaves of bread.

Sit them in groups of fifty He said,

So into these groups they all were led.

He blessed the loaves and fish as to heaven He looked,

And the disciples around to the many the food they took.

Now when all had eaten and were filled,

Twelve baskets of leftovers they did yield.

Ref. Luke 9:10-17

Debbie Girard

A Great Task

It began with nothing but a large mass,

But God set out to do a great task.

The first thing He did was to give light,

And there was darkness He called night.

Then He made a firmament which He called heaven,

And this was the second day of the beginning.

Now God made the fruitful land and was well pleased,

Then He gathered the waters and called them the seas.

Now this brought the third day to an end,

Then the fourth day did begin.

Then God made the sun for the daylight,

And the moon and the stars to shine at night.

Now when the fifth day was there,

God created the sea creatures and the birds of the air.

Next was the cattle and all creeping things on earth,

To all of these God gave birth.

Then in His own image, God made man,

To rule over the animals and all the land.

Then the female He did create,

To give the man a friend and mate.

Now all this brought the sixth day to an end,

Then on the seventh day, the Sabbath would begin.

Debbie Girard

Oil In The Vessel

A widow feared a creditor would take her sons,

She came to Elisha to see what could be done.

Elisha asked, "What have you in your house today?"

Just a jar of oil is what she had to say.

"Borrow vessels from your neighbors till there are no more,

Take them home, then you and your sons close your door."

Elisha told her to fill every vessel she got,

This she did till there wasn't another pot.

"Bring me another," she said to her son.

He said to her, "We do not have another one."

The oil ceased to flow, so she asked Elisha what to do next.

He said, "Sell the oil, pay the debt, and you all live on the rest."

Ref. 2 Kings 4:1-7

She Came To Jesus

In the house of a Pharisee, Jesus sat,

And a woman who was a sinner knew where He was at.

She came to the house, Jesus to meet,

With tears in her eyes, she stood at His feet.

On Jesus feet, these tears did fall,

With the hair on her head she wiped them all.

She kissed His feet and anointed them with oil so sweet,

And Simon could not understand why she so kindly Jesus did greet.

To Simon a parable Jesus did speak,

To tell why He took in this woman who was so meek.

She came to Jesus with so much love,

For the Son of the Father up above.

Even though her sins were very many,

Jesus forgave them, and now there weren't any.

Ref. Luke 7:36-50

Debbie Girard

Praise Him

Lord, you are truly the one and only,

You never leave me feeling lonely.

When there is no one to talk to,

I know I can trust in You.

No matter what problems come my way,

I know I can give them to you and say,

Lord these burdens I give to you, then see,

The Lord then, just sets me free.

And I remember to give Him thanks and praise,

For getting me through those rough days.

I kneel before Him with love in my heart,

Knowing He loved me from the start.

To share His love with others is where I'd like to begin,

For those lost souls, Jesus will win.

I'll spend my life serving Him always,

And give Him all the glory and praise.

And someday Him I will meet,

Upon that Heavenly golden street.

Debbie Girard

Lend An Ear

Now I have a story that I want you to hear,

So come on now and lend an ear.

It's the story of Jesus and what He'll do,

If you just do what He asks you to.

Now just let Him in your heart today,

He'll lead you safely all the way.

So come on now, hear what I say,

Ask Him to forgive you here today.

Tell Him you love Him and in Him believe,

And then your side He'll never leave.

So come on now, get your heart in gear,

He's here right now and it's free, you hear.

Now you love Him and He's loved you,

Wow, now you got a life that's new.

Love One Another

Let us love one another from deep within,

That love from Christ, those souls to win.

Let us care for one another,

That we may always help our brother.

When love is there and ever strong,

In one accord will be our song.

Our hearts will be all joined as one,

With Jesus Christ, God's precious Son.

Debbie Girard

Wondrous Pleasure

As I sat under the old oak tree,

The beauty of nature I did see.

Beyond was a brook, sparkling and bright,

Oh what a cool and refreshing site.

The trees standing tall reaching the sky,

As many different birds flew by.

The flowers blooming all around,

No brighter colors can be found.

A soft warm breeze that gently blows,

The bounds of nature no one knows.

The butterflies, animals, plants and things,

All Gods' creatures He did bring.

For us to view in wondrous pleasure,

And for always, we should treasure.

His Strength

A tree reaches out to touch the sky,

As if it is glad to be growing so high.

Higher, higher standing tall,

But still rooted, humble and small.

It doesn't slouch or look unfed,

But shows it has strength instead.

We too must be as this tree,

Reaching higher, the Lord to see.

Standing in His Word each day,

Knowing it helps us all the way.

Being glad we have the victory,

Even though we may not see.

We mustn't slump and feel sad,

Because the Lord has made us glad.

So let us lean on His strength today,

Being full of joy and praise all the way.

Debbie Girard

Time With The Lord

Time with the Lord is so precious,

Time with the Lord is so good.

Time with the Lord gives you fullness,

Spend it with Him like you should.

He'll give you joy and peace,

He'll give you time to rest.

And in His Word don't cease,

Take time with the very best.

In His love, you'll abound,

When in His presence, you stay.

His Spirit can be found,

When you're with Him every day.

Let us remember to pray,

Give Him all glory and praise.

Loving Him more every day,

Following Him and His ways.

Cries In The Night

A little child cries in the night,

Somehow it's lost it's only birthright.

Its chance to know the joy life can bring,

Has been destroyed without it beginning.

The little thumping of its' heart,

Is now being torn all apart.

The little body that's beginning to grow,

All the beauty and wonders it will never know.

These little loving and sparkling eyes,

That weep as its little body dies.

Those little hands that want to hold on,

To the love of someone who's caring and strong.

There will never be a pitter-patter of those little feet,

That poor little child so small and sweet.

Oh let us pray for compassion and love,

To save this little child of God from above.

Debbie Girard

This little child may be inside of you,

Crying in the night, "What will you do?"

Oh Lord we pray this very night,

Let this little one have its' birthright.

Communion

I sit at a table, shabby and old,

To drink from a cup made of gold.

To eat of bread passed around,

No greater meal to be found.

This may not be a grand buffet,

But it's the table of the Lord where I sit today.

It's communion time with the Lord,

To remember that day of old.

When Jesus died for you and me,

To set all of His people free.

Let us ponder on what it means,

As our hearts, we make clean.

Debbie Girard

Guide My Feet

I don't want this world's riches,

They don't mean a thing.

I just want your love Lord,

Your praises to sing.

Oh guide my feet Lord,

In the way, they should go.

And through Your Word, Lord,

Teach me what I should know.

Don't Lose Heart

For Christ there was joy that lay ahead,

Even though His blood had to be shed.

The pain of the cross He had to endure first,

While by sinful men, He was cursed.

But after the cross, the joy was great,

It held for everyone the ultimate fate.

Twas for our sins He bled and died,

That with Him we could abide.

We must have faith and Him believe,

A heavenly home we will recieve.

So first we also must suffer pain,

Because there is a joy we'll gain.

So abide in Him and don't lose heart,

For of Gods' family, we are a part.

So on Jesus focus your eyes,

And press on for the heavenly prize.

(Hebrews 12)

Debbie Girard

Angels Are Rejoicing

Listen with your ear,

There is a sound that you will hear.

It is the sound of the angels rejoicing,

Listen to the sounds of the singing.

Another soul has been won,

For the glory of the Son.

Praise the Lord, let us shout,

This is what it's all about.

For the joy this soul is bringing.

Heaven is ringing,

Hallelujah, praise His name,

He is forever and always the same.

The Mountain

Don't look at the mountain, look over the top,

If you look at the mountain, you'll only stop.

Look over the mountain and you will see,

What wonderful things there is going to be.

The Lord will lift you over it no matter how big it is,

Because He loves you and you are His.

So get up and on we go,

To a place where His glory, He'll show.

Debbie Girard

"Just For You"

I was a baby born in a manger bed,

Where all the cattle and sheep were fed.

I walked the earth from here to there,

Teaching people everywhere.

Then I knew what I must do,

I had to do it "Just For You."

With a whip they placed stripes upon my back,

So for your healing, you'd never lack.

The crown of thorns I had to wear,

All this pain I had to bear.

They mocked and scorned and laughed at Me,

Not even knowing I would set them free.

The nails in My hands, oh such agony,

On a rugged cross, they placed Me.

There I hung until I died,

While many people grieved and cried.

Placed in a tomb till the third day,

Then I arose to make the way.

Now the covenant was made new,

This I did, "Just For You."

Debbie Girard

He Holds The Key

It's a new time, a new start,

To change the feelings in your heart.

To open doors that lead the way,

For what the Lord has, beginning today.

He holds the key in His hand,

To give you all that He has planned.

Don't hold back, but step ahead,

By the Lord's hand, you will be led.

Don't worry or look behind,

The Lord will give you peace of mind.

The Eyes Of A Child

What do you see in the eyes of a child,

A love that is tender and oh-so mild.

A look of wonderment at things they see,

Or when they are grown who they may be.

A look saying Won't you please help me on my way,

Leading and guiding me every day.

They look to someone loving and strong,

Who'll teach them to stay away from all wrong?

With the Lord in your heart and a smile,

You can reach the eyes of a child.

Debbie Girard

The Shining Light

Though the night is dark and cold,

There is someone whose hand you hold.

Someone whose love is always there,

Saying to you, "I really care."

Just as a ship is tossed on a dark stormy night,

The strong lighthouse shines with a bright light.

To lead and guide you through the roughest hour,

He'll be there in His glory and power.

Though silence may fall all around,

You can feel His love and in it abound.

You And I Lord

You and I can make it Lord,

We can see this journey through.

You and I can make it Lord,

You will tell me what to do.

You are my strength and courage Lord,

You'll pick me up and lead my way.

You are my strength and courage Lord,

You are with me every day.

Thank you Lord for all Your love,

You mean so much to me.

Thank you Lord for all Your love,

You alone can set me free.

Debbie Girard

More Than.............

Lord You mean everything to me,

More than the oceans or the depths of the sea.

More than the highest mountain I have to climb,

More than the minutes and hours of time.

More than all the grains of sand you see,

More than life eternally.

Nothing in this world can ever take Your place,

You are all that I can embrace.

Thank you Lord for being You,

I want to love You in all I do.

Secrets

Life is full of cares and woes,

Where they take us no one knows.

This day's up, the next one down,

There is no calmness to be found.

I wouldn't want to know what lies ahead,

Cause then there'd be something for me to dread.

The best I can do is just to hang on,

And keep on moving with each new dawn.

It's best left in the Masters' hand,

Only on Him can you stand.

Debbie Girard

Why?

Why do people hurt each other so?

I guess that's something we'll never know.

Those cruel words can break a heart,

And place people far apart.

The tears that words cause one to shed,

Are better kept quiet than to be said.

Why should we cause this hurt to one another,

When we are to truly love each other.

What a blessing it would be if we were kind,

What wondrous friendships we could find.

His Sacrifice

There is no way to understand how Jesus withstood the pain,

While here on the earth He did remain.

While many came His face to seek,

There were others against Him did speak.

Miracles again and again He did show,

Yet there were some that Him they didn't know.

He knew the sacrifice He had to make,

The mocking and beating He had to take.

His love for us was so great,

It opened up heavens' gate.

Debbie Girard

Noah

In the Lords' sight,

Noah tried to do what's right.

Others laughed and made fun,

They thought Noah was kind of dumb.

Pairs of animals he went to find,

He needed two of every kind.

Into the ark, he put them all,

Then the rain began to fall.

He and his family were safe inside,

While people of the land had nowhere to hide.

The rain came down day after day,

Will it ever go away?

Forty days later it finally did stop,

And the ark sat on a mountaintop.

Noah let a dove go out of his hand,

To seek and find some dry land.

The dove came back, Noah to see,

Carrying a branch from an olive tree.

A rainbow was Gods' promise on that day,

That never again would a flood take the world away.

Debbie Girard

Reflections

When I spoke, what did I see,

Was it Jesus or was it me?

When I made a choice, was it right,

Was it pleasing in His sight?

When my actions took place,

Did I see Jesus' face?

When others laughed at a joke that was told,

Did I weaken in laughter or stay strong and bold?

When someone was hurting, did I put them down,

Or did I show where the love of Jesus is found?

When I see my reflection, I know what I want it to be,

I want it to always be Jesus and never be me!

The Rays of The Son

Behind a cloud, shaded gray,

There is someone to lead the way.

His presence may seem out of sight,

But it is there shining bright.

You may feel that alone you stand,

But He's reaching out, holding your hand.

See how the brightness of the suns' rays glow,

Oh all His glory to you, He will show.

Look up and see what's there for you,

It is such a precious view.

The light of the rays from the sun,

Reflect the glory of Jesus, the holy one.

Debbie Girard

His Love

He's reaches out His hand and takes hold of mine,

Somehow I know everything will be fine.

I go with Him, where I am led,

With His arm around me, "You're special," He said.

"I want you to go with me,"

I looked in His eyes, a treasure to see.

It was such a compassion and love seen there,

Something that had never been felt anywhere.

It's hard to express in words what it meant,

But I do know from heaven it was sent.

I felt such a peace deep inside,

I know in Him I will abide.

Thank You Lord for the love You showed me,

I know it's just a little of what I will see.

My Letter To Jesus

Dear Jesus, my love for you is so strong,

To you does my heart and soul belong.

You lead and guide me in good times and bad,

You are with me when I'm happy or sad.

When others hurt me and let me down,

You are there to turn things around.

Words can't say what You mean to me,

But my heart, I know You can see.

A simple "thank you" seems so small,

I know I must give to you my all.

Please take all the love for you in my heart,

And from your love, I will never depart.

Debbie Girard

Compassion And Grace

Today you see so much bitterness and hate,

Leading to a devastating fate.

Where people are rude and so unkind,

They have no love for mankind.

They fight with mouths and crude words,

With battle gear and with sword.

Will it ever stop or end?

Only with the love of Jesus, my friend.

I'm so glad the Lord is so full of compassion and grace,

His wondrous love you can embrace.

The depth of His compassion you can not see,

But it is always there for you, for me.

We know that He is always there,

Holding us in His tender care.

His kind of love is what we need,

In all our thoughts and words and deeds.

On His Wings Of Love

On the wings of His love,

A great gift sent from above.

Love so strong it never fails,

No matter what life entails.

When rough times you go through,

His love is always there for you.

In happiness and in sorrow,

His love is there today and tomorrow.

On His wings of love, you will prevail,

Because His love will never fail.

Debbie Girard

I'm Here, Don't Fear

All these fears and all these doubts,

What is this world all about?

My child do not worry,

This is not your story.

You are in this world today,

But I have made for you a way.

You gave your heart and life to me,

So of this world, you've been set free.

I'm with you each and every day,

To take your fears and cares away.

Have faith and trust in Me,

And the victory you will see.

A New Beginning

With each step I take, let Jesus lead my way,

Lead me where you want me to go, I pray.

This is a new year, a new beginning,

Let us praise you with voices singing.

Renew us in you O Lord,

Let us follow You closer and learn Your Word.

Walk with us and keep us in your care,

In this time when there is trouble everywhere.

Let us hold strong to our faith within,

And keep us pure and away from sin.

Though troubles can come from the left and right,

Let us hold to your love and hold on tight.

Though many trials can come our way,

Keep us in Your arms to stay.

Let us be faithful and strong,

Let us sing to you a thankful song.

To let you know we trust in you,

And with your leading, your work we will do.

With Love And Prayers

Hold on to your family with all of your heart,

This old world is trying to pull families apart.

Tell them all about the Lord,

Teach them from God's precious Word.

The sins of the world are rampant today,

They will try to lead many astray.

Please think of the children so small and sweet,

Let's lead them to Jesus, and they can sit at His feet.

All those that you know and love,

Should know of God and His home above.

Please pray for God to keep us safe and in His care,

To protect us from the evil that is everywhere.

Put all your trust in God today,

Have faith that He will show you the way.

Please pray with all of your heart,

So families and loved ones can't be torn apart.

Debbie Girard

Vessels In The Sea Of Life

We are the vessels in the sea of life,

Facing waves of sorrow and strife.

Vessels to carry and share the good news of the Lord,

Spreading the gospel and sharing His Word.

Our vessel should carry a bright shining light,

That others can see when we're in their sight.

When the sea is raging and we're tossed about,

God can calm the storm without a doubt.

He guides our vessel along the way,

As in Him we put our trust and obey.

A prayer sent up in the calm of night,

That our vessels stay on the path that is right.

On the sea of life, our vessel will go,

Spreading God's Word and letting it flow.

Gods' Way Not My Way

God says, "I am the Master, I am the guide,"

The path is narrow, it is not wide.

In todays world, they quote, "It is all about me,"

Wasn't it Jesus who set you free?

I want that and I want this,

It's His plan we sure do miss.

It should be, "God, what do you want today?"

His path is straight and He'll guide your way.

Get rid of the I, I, I,

And on our Savior, we should rely.

For He is the way the truth, the life,

Doing it my way will lead to strife.

My heart must change from me to you,

For Gods' will is what we need to do.

Lord take my life and hold my hand,

It is in you I want to stand.

Debbie Girard

The Journey

Jesus is born, His journey begins,

To save all His people from all of their sins.

As He travels the streets of the earth,

The child of that wonderful Christmas birth.

He searches for twelve men along the way,

That give their lives to follow Him every day.

He travels all over from here to there,

And people come to see Him from everywhere.

He talks of love and faith and grace,

They see His love upon His face.

Miracles He does, His faith sets them free,

The lame can walk and the blind can see.

His mission is to reach all the people He can,

This is all part of Gods' wondrous plan.

Jesus knew He faced many things ahead,

He knew His blood would be shed.

This He would do for you and me,

So we could walk with Him in eternity.

Debbie Girard

A Blood Stained Cross

There's a blood-stained cross where Jesus bled an died,

While those who were there knelt down and cried.

Two pieces of rugged wood He carried that day,

The reproach He bore to take my sins away.

I bow on my knees and cry out in shame,

For all of my sins, He took the blame.

His love for me is so great and vast,

That he can forgive my terrible past.

Lord I give my heart completely to you,

Come into my life and make me new.

Thank you Lord for loving me,

For cleansing me and setting me free.

I will remember the blood-stained cross you bore that day,

To take all of my sins away.

So Wonderful

He is the light in my heart,

I could tell it from the start.

He brightens every day,

That comes along my way.

He picked me up when I was down,

I once was lost but now I'm found.

I feel a joy inside,

And this I can not hide.

My joy I will share,

with others everywhere.

Yes let's bring them in,

Away from all the sin.

He will take away your sin,

If you will let Him in.

In your heart to stay,

He will help you every day.

Debbie Girard

Someday with Him you'll be,

Through all eternity.

To live forever more,

On that great and peaceful shore.

God is so wonderful,

Most wonderful of all.

Yes He is most wonderful of all.

Gift Of Love

Long ago on a special night,

There was a star that shined so bright.

A babe was born in a manger bed,

Where all the sheep and cattle were fed.

There in the town of Bethlehem,

Three wise men from afar they came.

They brought frankincense, myrrh, and gold,

To that small babe their love they showed.

To shepherds, angels came to say,

A Savior is born this very day.

Goodwill to men and peace on earth,

Come with this Christ child and His birth.

That babe is very special you see,

That babe was born for you and me.

The angels up in heaven above,

Told all of God's great gift of love.

And Jesus was that babys name,

That gift of love from God He came.

The babe born on that special night,

Sent to the world to make it right.

Just Like The Shepherd

The Lord has blessed me oh so much,

I praise Him for His loving touch.

More than I deserve He's given me,

He's given me love and set me free.

I was lost in the world somewhere,

He looked for me cause He did care.

I opened my heart and let Him in,

He cleansed me from all of my sin.

Have you praised Him for what He's done,

Look back to the blood of His Son.

We have not praised Him as much,

As the blessings He's given us.

So let us stand and give Him praise,

Every day, seek to see His face.

Show your love to Him each day,

In a very special way.

He set me free from a world of sin,

He gathered me up and led me in.

Just like the shepherd who gathers his sheep,

He brought me into His fold to keep.

Glad Tidings

"Tis the time of good wishes and lots of cheer,

To all those we know far and near.

A time to celebrate a most special night,

When one lone star shined so bright.

To bring glad tidings to one and all,

Of the birth of a child so tender and small.

His wondrous love so vast and great,

Brings you right to heavens' gate.

May the miracle of His love touch your heart,

And may you never from that love depart.

May the love and peace of this season be with you,

Today, tomorrow and the whole year through.

A Few Every Day Poems

For You To Enjoy

Love Dies In A Sea Of Lies

We had a love deep in our hearts,

But a sea of lies tore it all apart.

Love doesn't exist if you cause so much pain,

And then keep causing it again and again.

The vows made on our wedding day,

Are now lost and far away.

Gone now are the days of our love and devotion,

Lost in a sea of strange emotion.

The pieces are tossed from here and yon,

That love we had is forever gone.

All the trust that there had been,

Can never be found for us again.

There are no longer feelings there,

Because you showed you didn't care.

There are no tears left to cry,

In the sea of lies our love did die.

Debbie Girard

A Special Friend

Someone who listens and lets you know they are there,

Someone who doesn't criticize but lets you know that they care.

Someone who knows you are hurting inside,

Someone who shares the tears you have cried.

Someone who stands by you in what you decide to do,

Someone who knows that you care about them too.

It takes someone special to be a good friend,

And a friendship like that can have no end.

God Bless You

For all the brave soldiers willing to fight,

To defend our country and do what is right.

You stepped forward and took a stand,

To protect the freedom of our land.

Our hearts go out to those whose lives were lost,

Even though we know freedom comes with a cost.

We send our deepest thanks today,

God bless and keep you till you're home to stay.

Debbie Girard

Remember

Today we honor the courageous and strong,

In our hearts is where they belong.

They fought so this country could be free,

A legacy passed to you and me.

God has a wondrous plan,

For the people of this land.

If in Him we put our trust,

He will send His peace to us.

So let us all begin to pray,

That God will lead us every day.

To make this country free indeed,

So what many fought for will succeed.

We thank God for those who gave so much for this land,

Lord hold them gently in your hand.

Sweet Dreams

Close your eyes, go to sleep,

Not a sound, nor a peep.

You'll be safe while you rest,

Angels watching o'er your nest.

You are so loved, O loved so much,

It's in my heart and in my touch.

Dream of love, dream of peace,

Let your wonders never cease.

Life is full of little tests,

And you deserve the very best.

So take your time as you grow,

Before too long much, you'll know.

Now when you wake, I'll be right here,

Have no worry, have no fear.

I will help you every day,

Help you grow in every way.

Debbie Girard

So close your eyes, go to rest,

Dream a dream, the very best.

Hush-a-by, my little one,

sweet dreams to you.

Hush-a-by, my little one,

Sweet dreams come true...for you.

(written for my daughter when she was born)

Holiday Wishes To You

This is the time of year, you know,

When the ground is covered with new fallen snow.

When Rudolph is getting ready to go,

And Santa is practicing his jolly ho-ho.

The elves are busy with all of the toys.

That they're getting ready for good girls and boys.

Mom is busy doing her baking,

Look at all the goodies she's making.

And all the shopping that needs to be done,

To make this holiday so much fun.

But in all this rush, there's something I'd like to say,

And that's to wish all of you a happy holiday.

And May all the wishes you have for the new year,

Bring you many nice things and lots of good cheer.

Debbie Girard

A Teacher Thank You

T is for Teaching what children need to know.

H is for Helping the child to grow.

A is for Answering all the questions they have.

N is for Nervous, how you feel when they are bad.

K is for the Knowledge that you pass on to all.

Y is for Yelling when they run down the hall.

O is for Opening their minds to new things.

U is for Understanding the needs each child brings.

This is just to say "thank you" For a job well done. Teaching our children that learning is fun. Teaching when children are good or bad. For teachers, we're thankful and very glad.

Gone......

My life was torn, everything that mattered,

My hopes and dreams all were shattered.

What I had built through the years,

Now has left me with many tears.

The trust, the love we once did share,

Is gone forever cause he didn't care.

What there once was can not remain,

Because it vanished in the hurt and pain.

I must move ahead to what is new,

Whatever it may be, that I must do.

Debbie Girard

Changes

'Twas just a few days ago,

When it began to really snow.

A little flake here, a big flake there,

The flakes were falling everywhere.

'Tis time to get out my coat and hat,

And put away my ball and bat.

Changes come and changes go,

Just like the seasons, don't you know?

Days End

One summer day as I look at the hills,

Something out there, to me, appeals.

The sun is setting in bright array,

Calling the end to another day.

The colors reflecting the warmth of the air,

Dazzling the sky with vibrant flare.

The magic that only nature can give to all,

In the spring and summer, winter or fall.

The peace of the day nearing the end,

As nightfall comes and stars attend.

A time to rest in the still of the night,

While the moon and stars shine so bright.

And as our rest nears an end,

A new day is about to begin.

With the wondrous color it will start,

And in the magic we are again a part.